Original title:
Hawthorn Hopes

Copyright © 2025 Creative Arts Management OÜ
All rights reserved.

Author: Juliette Kensington
ISBN HARDBACK: 978-1-80566-750-6
ISBN PAPERBACK: 978-1-80566-820-6

Nestled Dreams in Prickly Arms

In the garden where the laughter grows,
A prickly hug that nobody knows.
With dreams a-dancing on each sharp edge,
We laugh out loud, take the silly pledge.

Petals whisper jokes to the winds,
While the sharp ones laugh at our silly sins.
A snail slides in, on a leafy spree,
"Why run from the thorns? Come party with me!"

Heartbeats of Thorny Essence

A rose so bold wears its fierce attire,
With thorns like bouncers, it knows the fire.
"Take a chance!" a brave bee said with flair,
Just don't mind the prickles; you'll get through there!"

Life's a dance on this thorny stage,
We trip and tumble and turn the page.
With giggles echoing among the leaves,
Nature knows laughter is what she weaves.

Portrait of a Bright Tomorrow

Carved in green, a picture unfolds,
With buzzing laughs and stories told.
"Tomorrow's bright, with thorns so spry!"
Shouted a squirrel, as it waved bye-bye.

The sun paints smiles on each leafy face,
In this thorny realm, we find our place.
Sketching joy on a canvas of green,
Where humor reigns and joy is seen.

Starlit Blooms and Thorned Paths

Under the stars, we chase our dreams,
Through paths of thorns, or so it seems.
Every step, we giggle and gleam,
"Who knew nature was such a team?"

With every bloom, a tale is spun,
Of the battles fought and the jokes won.
Thorns can tickle with their sharp little ways,
As we dance through night and greet the rays.

Barefoot on Petaled Dreams

In the garden, I lose my toes,
Stepping softly where laughter grows.
Petals tickle my silly feet,
As I prance around, quite a treat!

Butterflies giggle in the air,
I wonder if they notice my flair.
Each bloom winks, I wink back too,
A silly dance in morning dew!

Glistening Hues of Expectation

Colors splash like paint on glee,
Expectations bounce like a bumblebee.
In this garden of wild delight,
Every petal shines, oh, what a sight!

Lemons laugh, and oranges spin,
Knowing well, we all can win.
A rainbow tickles the azure sky,
While daisies debate, and tulips sigh.

Ascending Through the Thorns

Thorns are sharp, but I won't fret,
I'll climb up high, won't you bet?
With a goofy grin and a strong will,
I'll reach the top, what a thrill!

As I bounce on prickly trails,
I dream of sandwiches, and pails.
Who knew the climb could be this fun?
All the laughter, oh, I've won!

Blooming Amidst Adversity

Amidst the weeds, I strike a pose,
A dandelion, I am, who knows?
With a wink, I sprout so bold,
In chaos, there's magic to behold!

Challenges come, they poke and tease,
But I'm a flower with playful ease.
Watch me giggle, dance with delight,
Blooming brightly, oh what a sight!

Fragrant Promises in Bloom

Petals dance with cheerful glee,
Swaying wildly, come and see.
Bees are buzzing, sipping sweet,
While squirrels prance on tiny feet.

Colors splash like vibrant paint,
A garden's joke, so bold, so quaint.
Blooming laughter fills the air,
Tickling noses without a care.

Echoes of Resilient Roots

Deep below the soil, they hide,
Little whispers, side by side.
Poking fun at winds that blow,
"Try your best, we'll give a show!"

Roots like ribbons twist and twine,
Plotting pranks on sun and vine.
"Who's the strongest?" they all boast,
With a giggle, they toast.

The Thorny Path to Tomorrow

Stumbling on a prickly bit,
Laughing as we try to sit.
Each sharp turn, a funny fall,
Yet onwards we will still crawl.

With every step, a poke, a jab,
"A rose has thorns, it's just a fab!"
But through the prickles and the tease,
We'll find our way, just wait, with ease.

A Serenade of Silent Growth

Underneath the moonlit sky,
Roots are singing, oh so shy.
In the dark, they plot and scheme,
Whispering wishes, chasing dreams.

A stretch here, a wiggle there,
"Let's outgrow the neighbor's flair!"
Silent giggles fill the night,
As they grow with pure delight.

Beneath the Boughs of Hope

Underneath the leafy spread,
I found a squirrel dream in bed.
He wore a hat made from a pie,
And danced around, oh my, oh my!

Chirping birds joined in the spree,
While ants took turns, as brave as thee.
A bumblebee with glasses spun,
Said, "Trust no flower, but join the fun!"

The Dance of Spring's Revival

A bunny in a bright bow tie,
Jumps high to catch a cloud in the sky.
His partner, a chipmunk, quite the champ,
Dipped low and lit up like a lamp.

They twirled past daisies painting their shoes,
And called upon the bees for a rousing blues.
With every step, the blooms did sway,
While laughter echoed, brightening the day.

Fragments of a Blossom's Song

Petals whisper tales of cheer,
As dandelions spin, oh dear!
They spread their seeds like giggles bright,
And tickle noses in the daylight.

A garden gnome, with a grin so wide,
Rode a snail down the old hill slide.
"Good luck!" he cheered, onlookers stopped,
As flowers bounced and the giggles hopped.

Growing Where the Wild Roots Tangle

In a patch where wild things play,
A hedgehog danced the day away.
He wore a crown of twigs and grass,
And joked with crickets as they passed.

Roots intertwined like friends so close,
A laughing tree, proud like a host.
With mushrooms giggling at the sights,
They shared their dreams on wild spring nights.

Budding Life in Shadows of Steel

In the city of gray, a sprout took its stand,
Tickling the concrete, it waved with a hand.
A squirrel peeked over, ripped jeans on its tail,
Cracked nuts on the sidewalk, a comical tale.

A pigeon strutted by, in a shiny new coat,
Claiming the sidewalk, it fancied a boat.
With a puffed-up chest, it glared at the trees,
"Bring on the spring blooms, I'll take all the bees!"

A breeze whispered secrets, so silly and bright,
While flowers burst giggling, in colorful light.
They danced with the shadows, a zany kinda show,
As laughter erupted from plants down below.

So here's to the quirks, in this concrete we find,
Each bud with its humor, each bloom intertwined.
With joy in their petals, let's join in the jest,
In a world full of chuckles, a garden's the best!

Whispers of Fragrant Blossoms

In gardens where laughter hides,
Blossoms giggle as springtime rides.
Bees buzz with a ticklish spree,
Dancing 'round like kids set free.

Petals sway with a cheeky grin,
Chasing clouds like a game to win.
Each sunny ray a playful tease,
Nature's jest, a joyful breeze.

The Promise Beneath the Thorn

Thorns may prick, but oh what fun,
Underneath lies a sweetened run.
With brambles bold, we weave and twine,
A puzzle where surprises shine.

Berry stains on fingers bright,
Sipping nectar late at night.
Sneaky squirrels share a game,
Each playful leap, a moment's fame.

Dreaming in the Shade of Brambles

In shaded nooks where dreams take flight,
Snoozing under leaves, what a sight!
Whispers of breezes, secrets hold,
Tales of charm and daring bold.

Ants parade with a comical flair,
Climbing twigs without a care.
Underneath the watchful eye,
Of chipmunks playing hide and spy.

Petals Wrapped in Morning Dew

Morning wraps the world in cheer,
Dewdrops dance, a crystal clear.
Petals twinkle with each glance,
A morning show, a jolly dance.

With giggles wrapped in nature's arms,
Squirrels charm with silly charms.
Under blushing blooms so wide,
Each little moment, a joyride.

Resilience in the Wildflower's Embrace

In a field where daisies play,
A butterfly lost its way.
It danced in circles, quite a sight,
Chasing shadows in the sunlight.

The poppy laughed, the tulips stared,
"Dear butterfly, you seem quite scared!"
With petals bright, they gave a cheer,
"Join the party, have no fear!"

A bumblebee buzzed in delight,
Buzzing jokes that felt just right.
"Why did the flower wear a crown?
To be the queen of flower town!"

So in that wild and bright bouquet,
Life's mischief had a funny way,
Reminding all, with every prance,
In bloom, we find our silly dance.

Shadows of a Thicket's Heart

In the thicket, shadows played,
A squirrel's mask, a light charade.
With acorns flying through the air,
Each landing softly, what a scare!

The rabbit watched with twinkling eyes,
As laughter mingled with the sighs.
"Why so serious?" he did croon,
"Let's hop around beneath the moon!"

The hedgehog grinned, with spiky style,
Telling tales that made them smile.
"Why did I cross the leafy lane?
To find a joke, not just some grain!"

In that thicket, joy took flight,
Where shadows danced in pure delight.
With every punchline met with glee,
The heart of this wild home was free.

Echoes of Blooming Solace

In a garden where laughter sways,
Petunias joke through sunny days.
"Why was the flower late for tea?
It lost its petals, oh dear me!"

The lily chuckled, made a scene,
"Just bloom, my friend, it's all routine!"
With every joke beneath the sun,
The petals twirled, oh what fun!

The daisies came, a yellow crew,
Telling puns that just grew and grew.
"Why did the seed feel so spry?
Because it knew it could reach the sky!"

So in that garden, joy arose,
With echoes of giggles in all rows.
In blooming solace, life charmed us,
Amidst the blooms, we laughed, we trust!

Secrets of the Thorny Path

Along the path, the thorns would tease,
Crickets chirped with breezy ease.
"Why did the rose hide from the sun?
Too many selfies – it wasn't fun!"

A fox tiptoed, plotting with flair,
As thorns giggled, unaware.
"What do you call a thorny friend?
A prickly pal 'til the very end!"

Beneath the brambles, laughter bloomed,
Where secrets shared erased the gloom.
"Why did the thicket laugh so bright?
Because it knew the twist in the night!"

So wander there, and you will find,
A path of jest for the daring mind.
Embrace the thorns with open heart,
For in their humor, life plays a part.

Thorns and the Art of Growth

In a garden where few dare to tread,
Thorns laugh and dance above your head.
You tiptoe past with utmost caution,
But they just wave, quite full of passion.

With prickly jokes they prance around,
Each jab a tease, no need to frown.
Grow through the grief, as they say,
Let the thorns lead you on your way.

Heartstrings Tied to Blooming Branches

Attached to branches, oh what a sight,
My heartstrings pulled in wrong or right.
They sway and tug like a lively tune,
I laugh as I chase them under the moon.

Branches chuckle, so high and free,
Wrapping their humor around me.
When blooms burst forth in cheerful glee,
My heartstrings dance, oh, won't you see?

Echoes of an Unseen Garden

Whispers flutter through the air,
Echoes of laughter without a care.
In a garden where no one can peek,
Unseen blooms play hide-and-seek.

Their giggles traveled each winding path,
As sunbeams joined in on the laugh.
Nature's punchlines fall from above,
Each petal shines, it's a hidden love.

Nature's Poem of Hopeful Resilience

In the wild, resilience does spin,
Each leaf a grin, a cheeky win.
Nature pens verses on every tree,
Giggles of growth, wild and free.

Through storms and sun, they play their game,
With roots like jokes, they never feel shame.
Hold onto joy, let your spirit rise,
In the heart of the wild, laughter never dies.

A Tapestry of Budding Futures

Little buds peek out with glee,
Hands rub eyes, can it be?
Whispers of growth dance in the air,
Like secret dreams that we all share.

Bees wear tiny hats, it's really a sight,
They're debating nectar, oh what a fight!
Each bloom a joke, each leaf a laugh,
Nature's fun fest, a floral autographs.

Wind tickles petals, makes them sway,
They giggle softly, come out and play.
Roots playing hide and seek below,
What a silly game they've started to show.

Under the sun, the colors collide,
A patchwork of laughter that's well-supplied.
In every corner, a cheer erupts,
Budding futures in blooms, oh how they are chuffed!

In the Shade of Hopeful Twigs

Underneath branches, dreams do twist,
  Branches whisper, you get the gist.
A shadowy giggle floats in the breeze,
  Twiggy friends dance, all families tease.

Rabbits in bow ties throw a wild ball,
  While birds in tuxes attempt to enthrall.
A laugh on the breeze, shared without doubt,
  Tiny antics, oh what are they about?

Chirping and chattering, all is just fun,
  Leaves debating who's fastest to run.
Caught in the antics of nature's play,
Shade of the twigs, where mischief holds sway.

With every gust, new tales to unfold,
  In cozy shadows, joy never grows old.
Twigs are the guides in this playful spree,
  Hopes tucked away, like kittens in tree.

The Language of Blossoms Unspoken

In petals and leaves, humor is sown,
Each rosy blush, a joke of its own.
Daisies wear glasses, all quite refined,
Creating a scene that's truly designed.

Tulips might gossip about who is best,
As violets plot, putting gossip to rest.
Buzzing with laughter, the blossoms unite,
A secretive code hidden just out of sight.

They sway to an orchestra, petals entwined,
Comical costumes, deftly aligned.
Sunshine's applause for every mishap,
A floral affair as they all take a lap.

A language of petals, no need for a word,
In the garden of giggles, joy is preferred.
Unspoken laughter in colors that sing,
With each closing bud, a new joke takes wing.

Sunlit Resilience in the Underbrush

Beneath the sun, brave blooms appear,
With silly smiles, they banish all fear.
Feisty ferns fuss over the light,
While shadows giggle at this lovely sight.

Tiny critters with antics abound,
Rolling and tumbling, they dance all around.
A squirrel on stilts, a sight to behold,
Charming each leaf with a story retold.

In the brush where the sunlight beams,
Laughter erupts from nature's sweet dreams.
Each petal a punchline, each stem a quip,
A sturdy resolve in this meadow's flip.

Resilience found in the jests of the day,
As critters unite in their humorous way.
In sunlit embrace, they find their own voice,
A celebration of laughter, a shared happy choice.

Sprouts of Light Through Darkness

In shadows where the giggles grow,
Tiny sprouts have tales to show.
With sunshine peeking, oh what fun,
Even darkness dances, just begun.

Beneath the weighty, thorny cloak,
Laughter bubbles, and the branches joke.
They whisper secrets with a twist,
Tiny victories cannot be missed.

Wishes Sprung from Thorny Branches

From brambles come the wishes bright,
Each prick a tease, but what a sight!
A twist, a turn, a funny dance,
These thorns know well to take a chance.

With petals that poke and giggle loud,
They challenge all who dream aloud.
To pluck a wish from tangled vines,
A leap of faith in punchline signs.

The Beauty of Hidden Resilience

A smile peaks through tangled greens,
Where strength is found in quirky scenes.
These petals bloom in playful jest,
With every bump, a cheerful test.

Resilience wrapped in soft disguise,
Frolics forth in silly guise.
Through cracks and crevices, they pop,
With every blink, they just won't stop.

On the Edges of Blooming

At the brink of laughter's bloom,
With every poke, there's joy to loom.
The edges teeter, playfully wild,
With each new sprout, the world is riled.

A flip, a flop, a twisty cheer,
These blossoms giggle without fear.
On the edge, they sway and tease,
In every breeze, their humor frees.

Heartbeats Amidst the Greenery

In fields where laughter climbs so high,
The squirrels dance as clouds drift by.
With clumsy steps, I twirl around,
And trip on roots that hug the ground.

A bee buzzed by, quite out of tune,
As if it thought it was a cartoon.
It flew right into a flower's face,
And fell back dizzy from the chase.

The daisies giggle, petals wide,
While ladybugs take all in stride.
I joined them in a silly spree,
Pretending I was one of three.

Oh, how my heart beats like a drum,
In this bright world, all bright and dumb.
Each bump and bounce is pure delight,
In the green depths, my spirit takes flight.

Through the Gaps of Rustic Love

In a wooden chair, I sway with cheer,
Whistling songs that no one can hear.
The sun peeks through a curtain torn,
While I tell jokes to the corn mourned.

A chicken danced, slipped on the muck,
I swear it laughed, just out of luck.
The farmer grinned, his face aglow,
As the barn cat put on a show.

Old fences creak with tales untold,
In this crazy love, I feel so bold.
I ask the wind to share a laugh,
It whispers softly, "Take a path!"

Through every gap, a breeze does tease,
And nature chuckles with such ease.
Here in the rustic, time stands still,
With love and laughter, all that thrills.

Echoes of Fragrance in the Air

The roses giggle, quite a sight,
While daisies bloom in pure delight.
A whiff of mint lies in the breeze,
As butterflies perform their tease.

Amidst the blooms, a bee's mischief,
It buzzes loud, as if to sniff.
I swear it tried to take a sip,
And spun around to do a flip.

Petals fall, like laughter's sound,
While insects waltz upon the ground.
Each fragrance tells a joke divine,
In gardens where the sun does shine.

With each deep breath, a giggle shared,
Nature knows how to be unpaired.
An echo of fragrance fills the day,
Turning ordinary into play.

The Arbor of Forgotten Dreams

In an old tree, I found a seat,
Among the branches, soft and neat.
Birds debate on who can sing best,
While I sit back, enjoying the rest.

A raccoon sneaked, with snacks in tow,
Stole my lunch with a furtive show.
I laughed aloud, for who could blame,
This furry thief in a hat of fame?

Under the leaves, I pondered deep,
Counting dreams I dared to keep.
But shadows danced, full of surprise,
As giggles echoed 'neath the skies.

In this arbor, past and future swirl,
Where laughter twirls in a joyful whirl.
Forgotten dreams take flight, it seems,
In this crazy world of whimsy schemes.

Radiance Amidst the Unruly

In the garden of mischief, bright blooms sprout,
Wild antics arise, laughter's the shout.
With petals like giggles, they twist and sway,
Sunshine's a prankster, stealing the day.

A squirrel broke dance near the tulip's crown,
While daisies donned hats, the crows wore a frown.
Jellybeans rained down from clouds painted pink,
Nature's a jester, more fun than we think.

Threads of Serenity Intertwined

In a world full of chaos, yarns softly weave,
Laughing at worries, it's time to believe.
The wind tells funny tales of knots and ties,
As butterflies chuckle, they flutter and rise.

Spiders spin laughter in delicate webs,
Cats chase their shadows, like mischievous ebbs.
With every small stitch, the calm finds a way,
Whispers of humor brightening the day.

Whispers of Blossomed Dreams

Beneath the broad branches, dreams gently giggle,
With blooms like confetti, they dance and wiggle.
The bees tell secrets in buzzing delight,
While blossoms play tag, from morning to night.

A tulip told jokes to a bashful rose,
The sun snapped a selfie, as the laughter grows.
In secret the daisies plot pranks on the grass,
A carnival of laughter, where worries won't pass.

Beneath the Thorned Canopy

In shadows of thorns, where the wild things reside,
Laughter erupts like a cheeky surprise.
A hedgehog once tripped on a vine full of glee,
While thorns waved their arms, saying, "Join in with me!"

Come join the parade of the spiky and bold,
Where fun is the treasure, and friendship, the gold.
Overhead, a raven cracks jokes full of wit,
In this quirky haven, we're happier a bit.

Thorny Vines and Quiet Dreams

In the garden, vines entwine,
With prickles whispering, 'You're fine!'
I dance around with clumsy shoes,
While bees conspire to share their snooze.

The flowers giggle, colors bright,
I trip on petals, what a sight!
A snail waves slowly from his perch,
While daisies hold their laughing church.

But under leaves, the secrets hide,
Of tangled roots that twist and slide.
I pull a weed, it pulls me back,
And now we're in a playful snack.

So here I stand, a wondrous mess,
With thorny vines, I must confess.
I laugh with blooms, in light we play,
And watch the sun chase clouds away.

A Garden Beyond Reach

Oh, garden fair with greens galore,
I see the fruits, but can't explore.
The fence is tall, the gate won't budge,
I shake my fist — oh, what a grudge!

The veggies joke, they poke and tease,
'Catch us quick if you can please!'
I grab a trowel, swift and bold,
But slip and roll on soil, quite cold.

A rabbit laughs, 'You'll never find,
The treasure here, oh, never mind!'
I throw a carrot for the cheer,
And join the fun, the path's unclear.

With laughter ringing loud and bright,
I dream of veggies every night.
Though out of reach, I'll join the game,
In this wild garden, none's to blame.

Embracing the Shattered Light

The sun breaks through in quirky ways,
As shadows dance, in playful bays.
I trip on rays, a sparkling spree,
And butterflies all laugh at me!

Over here, a sunbeam slips,
And tumbles down with silly quips.
I chase the sparkles, round and round,
While giggles echo from the ground.

Each golden glint a teasing spark,
Makes daylight sounds that jump and lark.
I gather light like snappy glows,
And leave the worries where no one knows.

So here I stand in bright delight,
With shattered beams that shine so bright.
Embracing chaos, joy takes flight,
In every glance, a soft excite!

Echoes of Resilience in the Breeze

The winds remind me with their tease,
Of all the blooms that bend with ease.
They sway and twist, a funny dance,
With nature's whim, they take their chance.

A dandelion bows so low,
While thorns protest, 'Oh, let us grow!'
The rustling leaves laugh in the shade,
As nature's charm begins to fade.

A clumsy bird sings out of tune,
While petals wave beneath the moon.
I stand beside them, join the cheer,
For every laugh, I lose a fear.

With echoes ringing in the air,
I find my strength amidst the flare.
For in the breeze, we twirl and spin,
Resilience found, and joy within.

Blossoming in the Shade

In shadows where the giggles bloom,
A flower dances, making room.
With petals bright and antics wild,
It skips along, a playful child.

Beneath the trees, they twirl about,
Whispering secrets, giggling loud.
The sun peeks in, a curious spy,
While blooms compete for the bluest sky.

They craft a crown of woven glee,
With joyful hearts, they roam so free.
In this cool nook, the laughter flows,
Where every bud a joke bestows.

So come and join this leafy play,
In nature's shade, let's laugh away.
For in this world of greens and gold,
The funniest stories will be told.

Lanterns of Hope in the Thicket

In tangled brush, the lights ignite,
Like fireflies in the dark of night.
With every flicker, a new joke spins,
The lanterns laugh, and the fun begins.

A squirrel cracks jokes, with nutty flair,
While bunnies bounce without a care.
They chase the shadows, round and round,
As giggles echo, the joy unbound.

A raccoon steals a dance, oh so sly,
With every twist, he winks an eye.
These woodland wonders, a sight to see,
In thickets where laughter roams free.

So gather 'round, let the fun ignite,
In this thicket of hopes shining bright.
For amidst the green, where laughter flows,
The lanterns of hope forever glows.

Dreams Entangled in Nature's Thorns

In a garden wild, where thorns entwine,
A hedgehog dreams beneath the pine.
With prickly pillows, he spins and sways,
Crafting tales of the silliest ways.

The bees conspire with buzzing cheer,
Inventing new games throughout the year.
They tickle the flowers, a merry band,
While snickering petals lend a hand.

A turtle joins with a bashful grin,
In a race against time, he's ready to win.
But with every step, he trips and falls,
And laughter erupts, echoing through the halls.

So in dreams entangled, let's all unite,
In our thorny haven, with pure delight.
For amidst the prickles, fun shall bloom,
In this whimsical, nature-filled room.

A Mosaic Portrait of Flourishing

A patchwork canvas with colors bright,
Where giggles paint the day and night.
Each petal whispers a tale of cheer,
In this mosaic, fun draws near.

The daisies laugh, the roses twirl,
A dainty dance, a floral swirl.
They craft a painting, vibrant and bold,
Where every bloom a story's told.

A butterfly flits with a wink and smile,
Stirring up laughter all the while.
With wings of joy, it flutters high,
Painting the clouds in the big, blue sky.

So join this festival of blooming light,
In this lively mosaic, let's take flight.
For in every petal, a dream we find,
A masterpiece of laughter intertwined.

Unyielding Spirit Amongst Shadows

In the garden, shadows play,
Where giggling ghosts sway away.
With every twist, a joke does bloom,
A dance of light in the gloom.

Prancing bunnies, twirling bees,
Telling tales with rustling leaves.
An unwritten script, full of jest,
In the twilight, they surely jest.

A gopher grins, a hedgehog laughs,
As they plot their silly paths.
Through moonlit nights and sunny days,
Their antics spark in endless ways.

With a wink and a twist of fate,
These merry misfits celebrate.
In shadows deep, the fun won't end,
Unyielding spirits, they pretend!

Fragments of Light in the Dark

A firefly flickers, a beacon bright,
Dancing quickly, just out of sight.
Whispering tales, its glow unfolds,
Of playful nights and secrets told.

In moonlit cornfields, they shiver and sway,
Chasing shadows, they laugh and play.
The mischief spark in the evening cool,
The nightly game, a merry tool.

Squirrels exchange their nutty dreams,
In the glow of starlit beams.
With each bounce and hop, they declare,
Life's a jest, if you dare to care.

Fragments of laughter, scattered like seeds,
In pockets of joy, they meet their needs.
The darkness giggles, it's not too stark,
For in every shadow, a light does spark.

Silent Whispers of Hopeful Blooms

In a patch of dirt, a daisy spies,
The world around, where humor lies.
With petals wide, in dance so grand,
It's cracking jokes—oh, isn't it planned?

Lilies gossip as the sun arrives,
Their laughter, a song that surely thrives.
Each bud unfurls with a witty wink,
In gardens lush where dreamers think.

Weeds roll their eyes, with snickers deep,
As flowers bloom from their daylight sleep.
The earth chuckles, a comedic affair,
In whispers of hope, it plays without care.

With every breeze, a jest takes flight,
In this garden, the fun ignites.
Silent whispers bring laughter's tune,
Among the blooms, beneath the moon.

Navigating a Garden of Longing

In a vibrant plot, where dreams are weaved,
   Gardeners grin, though oft perceived.
They plant their wishes, sprout some cheer,
   With plots so wild, they persevere.

Gnomes take breaks, sipping tea with glee,
   Planning trips to the old oak tree.
With trowels in hand, they map their quests,
   While playful sprites hide in the nests.

The sun rolls in, a cheeky grin,
   Tickling the leaves, inviting them in.
With every step, a chuckle grows,
   Through tangled rows, the humor flows.

Navigating dreams, they dance along,
   In this quirky plot, where all belong.
With joyful hearts and hands in dirt,
   In every moment, they'll never hurt.

The Gold Beneath the Thorned Veil

In a garden where thorns do prance,
A berry bush invites a dance.
Socks on thorns? Oh, what a twist!
A treasure hunt none can resist!

Around the corner, laughter blooms,
With each poke, a giggle zooms.
Getting stuck? A fashion feat!
Who knew thorns could be so sweet?

A squirrel watches with a grin,
As I stumble and fall in.
But up I rise, with berry fame,
Next stop: a thorny obstacle game!

With every scratch, a joke is spun,
A riddle wrapped in prickly fun.
Yet in this patch, I find my gold,
A sweet surprise, and I feel bold!

Petals and Promises

Underneath the thorny arch,
A colorful petal parade does march.
With promises whispered on the breeze,
And a bee that teases with a sneeze!

One petal said, 'Let's ride a cow!'
While another claimed, 'I just love wow!'
A tumble here, a glimmer there,
In petal chatter, joy's laid bare.

So we giggle as we pile high,
A mountain of petals up to the sky.
Who needs a throne or a fancy dress?
In petal kingdom, we're all a mess!

A promise to reign with silly glee,
Amongst the thorns, so wild and free.
With each step, the antics unfold,
In a patch where laughter never gets old!

Where Dreams Take Root

In a patch where wishes sprout and play,
Dreams take root in a silly way.
Chasing after a feathered friend,
With a bounce in my step, no end!

Underthorned skies, I dare to leap,
Over puddles, where secrets keep.
Digging for treasure, though just a snack,
Oh, the surprises that dreams unpack!

With gumdrops growing on twiggy trees,
Every stumble brings a heartfelt tease.
In the thistles, the fun won't stop,
We'll dance on thorns and flip-flop!

So join me here, where dreams ignite,
In a patch of thorns that feels just right.
I'll plant a giggle, sow a grin,
In the muddled field, let's dive in!

A Tapestry of Thorned Colors

A tapestry woven with colors bright,
Thorns play tag in the fading light.
Each prick a giggle, each poke a cheer,
In this garden, there's naught to fear!

With twirling petals caught in a breeze,
And thorns that dance like mischievous tease.
We spin tales with laughter and delight,
A riot of colors in the fading light!

Painted dreams in shades so bold,
Every step, a story told.
With twigs for crowns and grass for shoes,
In this crazy patch, we cannot lose!

So let's create a funny scene,
A tapestry where life's so keen.
With chuckles wrapped in thorny strands,
In this vibrant land, joy expands!

The Resilience of Fragile Things

A tiny bud stands proud and bold,
While squirrels plot their acorn gold.
With petals soft, it greets the day,
A clumsy bee in disarray.

It sways and dances in the breeze,
Yet dodges raindrops with such ease.
It chuckles when the winds do gust,
In nature's game, it bounces, just.

Come winter's chill, it shivers slight,
Yet dreams of sunshine, warm and bright.
With every storm, it takes a chance,
This fragile thing knows how to dance.

So here's to blooms that brave the game,
With every twist, they stake their claim.
In laughter, light, and springtime's song,
These tiny things, they just belong!

Echoes of Spring's Heart

A crocus peeked from snowy bed,
"Surprise!" it winked, while others fled.
Amidst the frost, it sought the fun,
A party for the blooming sun!

The robin chirped a jolly tune,
While daffodils danced, all in full bloom.
They joked of winter, bold and brash,
"C'mon spring, let's have a splash!"

With blooms that mix bright yellow hues,
And playful winds that tease and cruise.
The garden laughs, in colors bright,
As petals twirl, a pure delight!

So here we stand, with hearts aglow,
As nature's glee begins to flow.
In every bud, a secret's known:
This merry time, we're not alone!

Thorns as Guardians of Dreams

The little rose, so sweet, so tamed,
Bears thorns that keep the tricks untamed.
A snail approached with dreams in tow,
"Dear thorny friend, why all the show?"

The rose replied with a gentle grin,
"To guard my heart from woes within.
For every dream, a thorn does sprout,
To keep the doubt and fears knocked out!"

The cactus chuckled, "What a plot!
Your prickly ways can save a lot!
In every bloom, a story told,
A jest of life, brave and bold!"

So here's to thorns, the guard and knight,
Who pave the way for dreams in flight.
With every prick, a giggle glows,
In the garden where the laughter grows!

Fluttering Hopes Amidst the Thorns

Beneath the thicket, a butterfly dreams,
In colors bright, with sunbeam gleams.
It flutters up, then dips down low,
Singing secrets only flowers know.

The thorns all snicker, "Look at her go!
She's dancing round like she's at a show!"
Amidst the pricks, it twists and twirls,
Defying bounds, in a world that swirls.

Among the thistles, its laughter rings,
A joyful tune that nature sings.
"No fear!" it shouts, in its playful flight,
"Even thorns can't dim my light!"

So let us skip through prickly lanes,
With hearts aglow and no refrains.
For every thorn that holds us tight,
There's freedom found in pure delight!

Petals of Promise in the Twilight

In twilight's glow, the petals dance,
Worn faces grin, given half a chance.
A squirrel rides a bike, quite absurd,
Chasing dreams in loops, it's never deterred.

Jokes bloom like flowers in the summer air,
As laughter spills forth from everywhere.
A bumblebee wearing a tiny hat,
Makes friends with a cat—imagine that!

Against the Harsh Facade

Behind the thorny mask, a riddle lies,
Where laughter erupts and the truth flies.
Grapes wear sunglasses, they'll never blush,
While the garden gnomes engage in a hush.

A tortoise finds its groove, gets up to speed,
With disco moves that could lead and succeed.
We'll paint the world with whimsy and cheer,
Ignoring the thorns that may linger near.

Threads of Ambition among the Thorns

In a patch where thorns might make you pout,
A group of ants struts loud, there's no doubt.
With tiny briefcases, they march in a line,
Dreaming of cheese—oh, how divine!

Threads of ambition weave stories right,
As snails sing ballads in dim moonlight.
One wears a crown of daisies so fine,
Planning board meetings by the old pine.

Anchor Points of a Spirited Journey

Each anchor point's a tickle of fun,
Where kangaroos play cards in the sun.
A wise old owl issues life's decree,
"Always pack snacks, it's the way to be!"

The road is a chuckle, full of twists and bends,
With flamingos in shades pretending to blend.
So come take a ride on this wobbly boat,
And let your laughter be the antidote!

Hues of Promise Amongst the Thorns

In gardens wild, a tale unfolds,
With blooms so bright, yet spiky holds.
A bee in flight, oh what a sight,
Amidst the thorns, it's pure delight.

A cheeky grin on petals' face,
While thorns prepare for an embrace.
"Hey, watch your step!" the flowers say,
As laughter swirls, and jokes at play.

The gardener trips on tangled roots,
While jesters dance in thorny suits.
With every prick, a giggle shared,
In this absurdity, we're all ensnared.

So raise a glass to prickers bold,
Where comedy and colors unfold.
For in this patch of wild delight,
We find our joys, oh what a sight!

The Thistle's Dance of Desire

In fields of mischief, thistles sway,
With twirling moves at end of day.
A dance of sharp, yet oh so bright,
  They tease the sun until the night.

"Hey, prickly friends, shall we unite?"
They laugh and twist in pure delight.
With petals soft and stems so tough,
  Their dance is odd, but never rough.

A rogue bird chirps, provides the tunes,
While thorns keep time, beneath the moons.
"Don't poke me!" cries a daisy fair,
  Yet joins the dance with flair and care.

So come and join this strange charade,
Where laughter grows and fears just fade.
In thistles' grips, we learn to prance,
  And find the joy in every chance!

In Search of the Unseen Dawn

When morning breaks with sleepy eyes,
The thorns conspire, a sweet disguise.
They stretch and yawn, their prickles bold,
As if to say, "We do what we're told."

A crow caws loud, a goofy song,
Echoing where the blooms belong.
The sun peeks through with rays of fun,
Yet thorns just wink, "We're not yet done."

They hide the light with silly poses,
While daisies giggle, blush like roses.
"Who needs the dawn?" they say with glee,
When twilight's antics set them free?

So join the thorns in jest and cheer,
For every dawn brings joy so near.
In nature's prank, we find our way,
Embracing all, come what may!

Hidden Hopes in Thorny Shadows

In shadows deep, where thorns reside,
A mystery blooms, no need to hide.
With misfit dreams and hopes uncurled,
They poke and prod, embracing the world.

A hedgehog strolls, with tiny grin,
As thorns look on, where laughter's been.
"Keep it down, please!" the roses plead,
While thorns just chuckle, planting seeds.

A fox in boots, quite out of place,
Prances through in this comical race.
"Can you find the hope?" they quirk their thorns,
While daisies shout, "It's in the morns!"

So let us wade through prickles bright,
And hold those dreams that feel just right.
For hidden joys in shadows play,
Bring smiles to hearts in every way!

Fragile Blossoms

Petals whisper secrets in spring air,
A clumsy bee buzzes without a care.
Tickled by giggles from nearby trees,
Nature's comedy, please take a seat.

In the garden, blooms play peek-a-boo,
With colors bright, like a cheerful crew.
Sunlight dances on the verdant floor,
Even the grass seems to laugh and roar.

A squirrel prances with a nut so grand,
Seems he's the king of this little land.
But trips and stumbles steal his fine flair,
Nature's jesters without a single care.

Softly they bloom, full of mischief and cheer,
Whispering wishes, we all long to hear.
In this vibrant world, every flaw is okay,
A funny reminder to seize the day.

Bold Aspirations

In the shade of trees with dreams so wild,
A daring rooster struts like a proud child.
Breaking barriers with each goofy pose,
He's got the strut, but not the right clothes.

The chickens giggle, they roll on the ground,
Chasing bold dreams that know no bound.
With feathers fluffed high and heads held so proud,
They flap their plans beneath the loud crowd.

Down by the fence, the goats start to plot,
A scheme for adventure, they've got it a lot.
With their horns held high, ready to try,
Falling sideways, they laugh at the sky.

Each day's a new chance to dance and to twirl,
In a world where every creature can whirl.
Chasing bold aspirations, silly and bright,
In this pasture of dreams, everything's right.

Shadows of Resilience

Under the moonlight, the shadows play tricks,
A turtle and rabbit form silly mix.
They waddle and hop with such odd grace,
In a nocturnal dance, they pick up the pace.

The snails cheer them on, with slimy delight,
Rooting for champions in the pale night.
With shells like helmets and hearts full of fight,
Every slow step turns into a might.

Beneath a small tree, a wise owl gives space,
To the chaos unfolding with spark and with grace.
Claiming resilience in the oddest of ways,
Creating sweet laughter in whimsical plays.

In the quiet of night, when the world feels dull,
Shadows remind us to embrace the full.
With joy in each stumble, their paths intertwine,
In a world of resilience, it's perfectly fine.

The Color of Lost Wishes

In the distance, a dandelion flies,
Wishes once bright now wear disguise.
A gust of wind turns dreams into spice,
Transforming the mundane into something nice.

Floating away are the hopes of the day,
A silly parade in a whimsical way.
Children chase laughter with eyes full of glee,
While wishes play tag, so wild and so free.

Each petal drops laughter like confetti in air,
As thoughts of the lost ones dance everywhere.
With every pluck bringing memories old,
Stories unfold, both funny and bold.

In the garden of dreams where wishes collide,
Life's color seems brighter with laughter inside.
Each lost aspiration, a treasure of sorts,
In this comedy of life, each heart supports.

Thorned Embraces in Spring

Beneath the roses, where prickles do dwell,
A hedgehog decides to throw a grand swell.
He wiggles and squiggles, a prickly parade,
In a bard's tale of wonder, adventures are made.

Thorns whisper sweet nothings to the breeze,
While ants march in rows, through the thorny trees.
One tiny ant trips, causing all to fall,
And laughter erupts—oh, it's a free-for-all!

Bees watch the chaos, with glee in their buzz,
Overhearing the shenanigans of was.
Every thorned embrace holds a secret inside,
A quirky connection that nobody can hide.

As springtime unfolds with a chuckle in tow,
Nature's odd friendships flourish and grow.
In this patch of hilarity, joy tightly clings,
With thorned embraces, true laughter it brings.

A Haven Amongst the Brambles

In a patch of brambles, quite the surprise,
A squirrel dances with sparkly eyes.
He trips on a twig, gives a comical shout,
And rolls in the roses, oh what a rout!

The bees wear sunglasses, sipping sweet tea,
While rabbits in top hats dance wild with glee.
A hedgehog in slippers cartwheels around,
In this bramble haven, joy knows no bound.

Beneath all the thorns, laughter is king,
With flowers that giggle, they start to sing.
Amidst the spiky and prickly despair,
It's the quirkiest club—everyone's there!

So if you feel lost in the prickly thicket,
Join this merry troupe, don't be a bit picky.
For laughter can flourish, despite all the thorns,
In the brambles of life, the silliness warms.

Sowing Seeds of Tomorrow

A seed in the ground, a curious sight,
Wonders and wiggles, oh what a fright!
"Am I a flower or a spunky weed?
Let's sprinkle some silliness, that's what I need!"

The veggies debate with their leafy attire,
"Who's the best sprout?!" sparks a wild fire.
Tomatoes all blushing, they're ripe for a fight,
While peas roll on laughter, in pure delight!

With carrots in capes, and radishes bold,
They plan a dance party, as stories unfold.
"Let's dance through the soil, instead of the rain,
Those pesky garden gnomes—let's give them a bane!"

So if ever you wander through rows of green dreams,
Remember the giggles and quirky little schemes.
For every dull moment can grow into cheer,
Just plant a bit funny, and dear joy is near.

In the Garden of Twisted Dreams

In a garden where giggles and shadows collide,
A rabbit in pajamas takes daring strides.
He tickles the daisies, they bursting with fun,
While the cacti complain, "This isn't how we run!"

There's a clock that's melting, a sight to behold,
It whispers to flowers of secrets untold.
The daisies are blushes, the violets giggle,
As the thyme on the window begins to wiggle.

In this twisted garden, where oddities bloom,
The gnomes paint the fences, creating a room.
With lanterns that chuckle and fireflies dance,
Even weeds join the party, given a chance!

So step through the gate where the wild things play,
In a garden of dreams, let your worries sway.
For laughter can twist every shadowy seam,
And create a haven, in this odd, funny dream.

The Thorns and Their Tender Tales

In the forest of thorns, where laughter prevails,
The bramble brigade spins whimsical tales.
A thistle once told of a rose with a mission,
To dance with the daisies in bright, joyous vision.

A cactus recounted the time of a bee,
Who wore tiny sneakers and said, "Watch me flee!"
He buzzed and he zigzagged, full of good cheer,
While thorns joined the laughter, "Hey, bring us a beer!"

The barbs have a wisdom, misunderstood maybe,
That sharp can be funny, it's often quite daisy.
They gather for stories beneath the bright moon,
Finding joy in the thickets, a jolly festoon.

So if you stroll past where the prickly ones dwell,
Listen close to the stories they whisper so well.
For even the thorns have their delicate dreams,
In the laughter of nature, enchantment redeems.

Secrets Woven in Petals

In the garden of whispers, secrets bloom,
Tiny petals giggle, in bright afternoon.
Bumblebees gossip in their buzzing spree,
While daisies wear hats, just to join the glee.

A ladybug winks, by the rose so bright,
Telling tales of love, under soft moonlight.
The sunflowers chuckle, heads all in a spin,
They plot mischief with the breeze, so let the fun begin.

Caterpillars dance, in their polka dot suits,
Hiding from spiders in their furry boots.
While ants play cards, and the crickets sing,
Nature's little jesters, oh, what joy they bring!

So here in this patch, where laughter is spun,
Every petal's a secret, in games just begun.

The Dance of Hopeful Branches

Branches sway joyfully, a comedic show,
As squirrels in ties put on a high-flying blow.
Leaves burst in laughter, they giggle with glee,
Whispering secrets, 'Can you dance like me?'

Wind plays conductor, and the birds take flight,
Chirping out jokes from morning 'til night.
With every flutter, a new thought appears,
Nature's own stand-up, scattered with cheers!

Bees join the line, with their buzzy parade,
Every flower's a friend, in this fun masquerade.
From acorns to blooms, all join in the jest,
Dancing through seasons, they give life their best.

So climb up the branches, join the wobbly dance,
For in this great theatre, we stand, take a chance!

Where Thorns Meet Light

Amidst prickly dwellers, a tale unfolds,
Of laughter and shadows, and stories retold.
Thorns wear a grin, poking fun at the sun,
While daffodils giggle, inviting everyone!

With cheeky little blooms, in colors so bright,
They joke with the thistles, 'We're quite the sight!'
Even the clouds can't help but to laugh,
As they drift overhead, a fluffy caricature graph.

The morning dew chuckles, as it glistens and shines,
Like a wink from a friend, adorned in designs.
Together they dance, with delight in the air,
Where light meets the thorns, there's fun everywhere!

Join in the frolic, where laughter takes flight,
In a world of sharp edges, they twinkle with light.

Budding Futures in a Thorny World

In a prickly little patch, new dreams start to grow,
Bud after bud, putting on quite a show.
With a flourish of petals, they tease the old thorns,
"Hey, look at us shine!" is the challenge that adorns.

Every new flower has a story to tell,
Of friendship with thistles, of laughter that swell.
Even under pressure, they dare to burst free,
In this jovial garden, they giggle with glee.

Sunbeams peek in, sharing warm little jokes,
While shadows play tag with the cheeky little folks.
Budding futures dance in a whimsical swirl,
In a thorny world, there's magic to unfurl!

So cherish each bloom, and the laughs that they bring,
For life's too short not to jump in and swing!

Rebirth Under the Canopy

Beneath green leaves, a squirrel prances,
   A dance of joy in playful glances.
A bird squawks loud, in a feathered suit,
   Chasing dreams of acorns, oh what a hoot!

The sun peeks through, a light-hearted thief,
Painting the ground with gold—what a relief!
A worm wiggles up, says, "Hey, take a look!"
"I'm writing my memoirs, it's quite the book!"

With laughter of breezes and petals that tease,
   Nature's giggles float softly on the breeze.
Each rustle and chuckle, makes no sense at all,
   In this leafy playground, we merrily sprawl!

So come find your glee, beneath this grand shade,
   Where every tiny creature's unafraid.
   Unity found in the strangest of sights,
   A whimsical world of joyous delights!

Nature's Quiet Sanctuary

In a cozy nook where insects hum,
Ants march in line, oh what a fun drum!
A grasshopper jokes, with one leg in the air,
While a butterfly sighs, 'Life's never a dare!'

Sunbeams like giggles peek through the trees,
Kissing the ground, stirring up the breeze.
A snail slides by, thinks he's winning the race,
While a chubby old frog's just munching on space.

Clouds float above, like pillows on high,
While the shadows watch, with a curious eye.
Each blade of grass waves a green little flag,
Whispering secrets that make nature brag!

So gather your thoughts in this serene space,
Where laughter and whispers dance in the grace.
Amidst the calm, hear the silly songs sing,
In Nature's sanctuary, we smile and swing!

Veils of Floral Ambitions

Blossoms in hats, all dressed up in style,
Competing for sunbeams, it's quite the trial.
Petals gossip grand, about bees in the air,
While dandelions plot how to give them a scare!

A tulip turns pink, in a fit of delight,
While roses roll eyes, in a bloom-fueled fight.
Lavender grins, in a sweet scented tone,
"I'm the best-smelling guest, leave me alone!"

The daisies form clubs, with their heads held so proud,
Creating petal crowns, laughing loud in a crowd.
Each bloom is a star, on a botanical stage,
Reciting their tales on this flowery page!

So come and join in, with your joyful heart,
In this garden of dreams, let's all take part.
With vines that entwine to create a fine show,
Where petals and laughter truly steal the glow!

Thickets of Unseen Possibilities

Frogs leap through shadows, springing from dreams,
While crickets compose, with their nighttime themes.
A rabbit proclaims, with a twitch of his ear,
"This thicket is splendid—come play over here!"

Branches all whisper, with secrets to share,
Of treasures and troubles that linger in air.
A curious fox, with a look oh so sly,
Winks at the moon, as it floats on by.

The thorns play the jester, all prickly and cute,
While mushrooms give shade, wearing hats like a brute.
Beneath the thick cover, adventures await,
With every step forward, we dance with our fate!

So let's revel in wildness, embrace the surprise,
In thickets where laughter and joy truly rise.
With each rustling leaf, hear the giggles anew,
In the heart of this chaos, find what's meant for you!

Shadows Play in the Garden of Ambitions

In a garden where shadows prance,
The weeds have all learned how to dance.
They giggle and twist, oh what a sight,
Even the flowers can't keep it polite.

The sun shines bright on ambitions bold,
But those pesky bugs think they're gold.
They munch on the dreams without any fear,
While the garden gnomes just stand there and sneer.

With every sprout, a tale to tell,
Of daisies that married a freakish snail.
A sunflower's wink, a tulip's sigh,
In this zany plot, even weeds can fly!

So here's to the laughter that blooms all around,
Where hopes twist and turn, oft' upside down.
In the wildest of gardens, let's join the fun,
For shadows of laughter have barely begun!

Petal-scented Promises

Under the blooms with vibrant flair,
Petals sway, promising a laugh to share.
Amidst the scents of sweet delight,
A bee hums a tune, oh what a sight!

The daisies gossip, their petals aflutter,
While roses flirt with each other, so utter.
A daffodil snickers at a passing bee,
"Do you dance like that? Oh, let's wait and see!"

Promises fragrant, with each gentle breeze,
Tickle the noses of bumblebees.
They buzz with mirth, as if on a quest,
Searching for nectar, they simply jest!

Petals of laughter fall soft to the ground,
In this garden, joy is happily found.
With whispers of fun carried on the air,
Each sweet promise ruffles up without care!

From Thorned Origins to Aspirational Heights

From a thorny past, a rose dared to dream,
With aspirations high, it plotted a scheme.
"Oh, I'll show them!" it said with a grin,
"In the garden of glory, I'll surely win!"

The daisies giggled as they watched it grow,
"Can thorns be funny? Oh, tell us, would you know?"
"I may be prickly, but with a heart so bright,
I'll tickle your petals, make the world feel right!"

As buds unfurled, dreams danced in the air,
With laughter resounding, the garden did care.
A waltz of florals, each step was a cheer,
From thorned origins to heights far and near.

So let's raise a glass to the quirky and wild,
For in every garden, there's a silly child.
From thorns to blossoms, our laughter ignites,
In the dance of the flowers, our spirit takes flight!

The Journey of a Blossoming Dream

A dream took root in a patch of sun,
With giggles and wiggles, it started to run.
It squirreled away with a twinkle of eyes,
"Let's soar to the moon!" it cheerfully cries.

Through dirt and muck, it stumbled and bounded,
With each tiny sprout, sprightly moments rounded.
"The world is a stage, let's put on a show!"
Said a cheeky old acorn, keen to grow.

With every bobble, each tumble and slip,
The dream learned to dance on an imaginary trip.
And oh, how it chuckled when clouds rumbled near,
"Rain is just laughter that tickles, my dear!"

So come join the dream, it's fanciful and bright,
With blossoms and giggles, it's pure delight.
From whispers to roars, let your humor gleam,
In the garden of life, let's chase every dream!

www.ingramcontent.com/pod-product-compliance
Lightning Source LLC
Chambersburg PA
CBHW051636160426
43209CB00004B/677